Right@Sight

a progressive sight-reading course

Violin Grade 4

Caroline Lumsden

EDITION PETERS

LEIPZIG · LONDON · NEW YORK

£6.95

Preface

Sight-reading is one of the most important yet neglected aspects of learning an instrument. If treated as an integral and enjoyable part of teaching from an early stage, it is easy to achieve considerable success. The *Right@Sight* series for violin and cello, developed by Caroline Lumsden and Anita Hewitt-Jones, is a very thorough approach that, if followed systematically, will produce excellent sight-readers and will more than prepare students for their graded examinations.

Right@Sight Violin Grade 4 is divided into 2 sections: section 1 (grade 4 – easier) and section 2 (grade 4 – harder). These sections are designed to help students progress smoothly from one grade to the next. A student completing both sections 1 and 2 before taking a grade 4 examination will be supremely confident at sight-reading.

Throughout this book, each double-page spread has a page of solo examples with helpful hints, followed by a page of duets to play with a teacher or friend. Students are encouraged always to use the mnemonic **TRaK** before sight-reading any piece:

> **T**ime signature: always check the time signature of a piece
> **R**hythm: clap the rhythm while saying the time names or singing the note names
> **and**
> **K**ey: always check the key signature of a piece and check what finger pattern is needed for that key

There are also *On your own* sections, containing pieces similar to those presented in the exam room – i.e. without any tips.

Encourage pupils to sing with note names – e.g. D E Fs (pronounced "efs"). All sharps have an "s" sound after the note and all flats an "f" sound (e.g. Bf is pronounced "beef"). Good intonation then becomes second nature.

To encourage rhythmic playing, particularly with young children, saying the rhythm in words can help to achieve real success:

Time names	Symbols		Time names	Symbols
slow	♩		trip-le-ty	3 ♪♪♪
ssh!	𝄽		sh!	𝄾
quick quick	♫		snap-py	♪ ♩.
semiquaver	♬♬		snap-py and	♪♪♩
quick-semi	♩♬		compound time names	
semi-quick	♬♩		slow	♩.
slow-ow	𝅗𝅥		slow-ow	𝅗𝅥.
slow-ow-ow	𝅗𝅥.		quick-e-ty	♪♪♪
slow-ow-ow-ow	𝅝		quick-er and	♪.♪♩
slow-er and	𝅗𝅥. ♪			
quick-er	𝅗𝅥. ♩			

Contents

Acknowledgements

Thanks go to Kate Allott, Kaat van Bouwel, pupils of Trinity String Time
and Charlie Denton for road testing the material.

Cover design by Adam Hay
Music setting by Robin Hagues
Printed in England by Halstan & Co., Amersham, Bucks.

Solos

Follow the **TRaK**

1 **T** The time signature shows how 4/4 can be grouped into 3+3+2 quavers when playing a **rumba**.

R Clap this, accenting the 1st, 4th and 7th quavers.

K How many sharps does A major have? Play the 2 octave scale.

Keep this very rhythmical and dance-like.

! Watch for the 3rd finger C♯ and G♯ in the lower octave.

2 **T** What is the time signature? Note the syncopation.

R Clap the rhythm carefully. Watch for the tied notes!

K Which two bars have both third finger D♮ and G♯?

! Remember to prepare the low 3rd finger C and G♯s

Emphasize the off-beats as you play through in a spirited, dance-like manner.

Duets

3 What is a **Courante**? What does *poco a poco* mean?

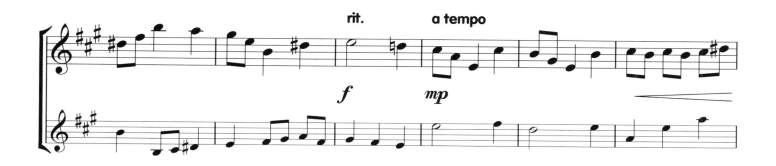

Solos

Follow the **TRaK**

4

T What other way could you write 4/4?

R Tap and say the note names in rhythm on the violin before playing.

K How do you know that the key is A minor and not C major?

? Which bar uses the harmonic minor finger pattern and which two bars the melodic minor?

Look ahead at the accidentals before playing. Perform with feeling.

5

T Why are there only three quavers in the last bar?

R Clap the rhythm carefully. Don't be caught out by the rests.

K Look at the chromatic passage (bars 9–11) and work out the fingering before playing.

Keep this short and rhythmical in the middle of the bow but not too fast.

! Watch out for string crossings.

Duets

6 Play this expressively, always listening to the rhythm of the 2nd part.
Be prepared for the stretch from the flattened 6th to the raised 7th.

Where is there a chromatic passage?

Solos

Follow the **TRaK**

7

T Why does the last bar only have two beats?

R How many times does the rhythm *quick–slow–quick* appear?

K Name the flats in the key signature.

? What does the accidental at the end of bar 3 tell you?

Play musically, observing all expression marks.

! Be ready for the shift to 3rd position. Where do you shift down again?

8

T What is the time signature and on what beat of the bar do you start?

R When playing, let the rhythm flow as if you were dancing.

K What key does this start and end on and what does it reach in bar 15?

Play expressively, using a bow to a bar for the slurs.

! Watch for the 4th finger Ebs and the shift to 3rd position.

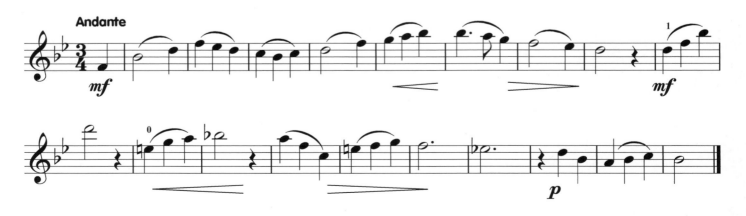

9 *What is a **Siciliana**?*

Note the 3rd position section and where you shift back to 1st position.

Solos

Follow the **TRaK**

10
- **T** What is the time signature and where are there ties?
- **R** Clap very rhythmically with note names i.e. G B♭ D G …etc.
- **K** Play the two-octave arpeggio of G minor twice.

Really emphasize the beat, rather like a 'rock' song.

11
- **T** What beat of the bar does this start on?
- **R** Clap the rhythm carefully, especially the first 2 bars.
  How many times does this rhythm happen?
- **K** Name the flats in the key signature.

Make this playful, with a contrast between sections.   **!** Watch out for accidentals.

Duets

12 *Play the scale of G melodic minor before you start. Note the time signature. Play smoothly and expressively with a feeling of 2 in a bar.*

Legato e espressivo

13   **T**   How many beats in a bar?

  R   Keep a feeling of 2 in a bar when you play.

  K   What is the key? Watch for the accidental in bar 6.

  ?   Where do you shift down to 1st position?

  !   Watch for the jump to 3rd position in the penultimate bar.

Play with a sweet tone, using two bows to a bar, letting the music flow.

Allegro ma non troppo

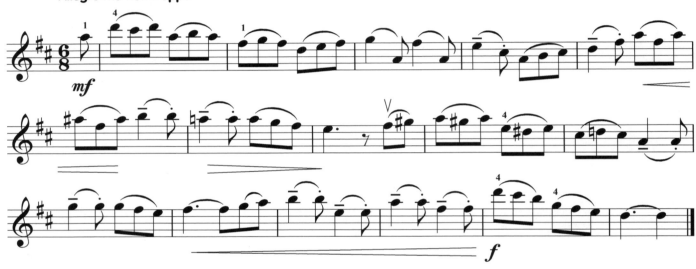

14   **T**   Which beat of the bar does this start on?

  R   Clap bars 1–4 taking care with the dotted and tied notes.

  K   Check the fingerings carefully, especially when in 3rd position.

  ?   What does **Lento espressivo** mean?

Use lots of bow as you play through very expressively.

  !   Be prepared for the slurred bowing across strings and the double stops!

Lento espressivo

Duets

15 *Entertain with this piece! Look ahead.*

Solos

16

T What is the time signature?

R Clap carefully with note names.

K What is the key and what is its relative major?

? Which bars have accidentals?

What does **Mesto e lento** *mean?*

! Play the two-octave scale of D harmonic minor before playing through.

17

T What is the time signature?

R Clap the first bar before deciding on a speed.

K Where is there a D minor arpeggio?

? What is the term given to the last chord of a minor piece that becomes major?

Play with spirit. Lift your arm right off after the pizz. chord to let the last note ring.

Duets

18 *Check all the accidentals before you begin.*

Don't be caught out by the rhythm in bars 3 and 11. Play through firmly, looking ahead to the position changes and double stopping.

Time Rhythm and Key

Solos

Follow the **TRaK**

19 **T** What is the time signature and how many beats do you count on a dotted crotchet?

R Accent the 1st beat of the bar to help this swing in quintuple time.

K What key is this in and where does it modulate to the dominant?

Make a real difference between f and p.

! The second section has fingering for 2nd position. Watch for the shift in bar 9.

20 **T** What is the time signature? How many bars don't have *quick-semi*?

R Clap the rhythm carefully.

K What key does this start in and what key does it end in?

Play this in a lively and spirited manner.

? What is a **Polonaise**?

16

Duets

21 Before playing this duet, play the top octave of C major in 2nd position. What finger pattern do you use? Now find your starting note. What do you think restez means? Follow the dynamics carefully and watch for the 'snappy' rhythms. Swap parts. Which is easier to play?

Solos

Follow the **TRaK**

Remember to check the TRaK as you play through the following examples on your own.

T Look at the time signature. When you have decided how fast to play, keep a steady beat.

R Clap the rhythm, then try any tricky bits on their own. Count carefully and don't try to play too fast.

K The key signature tells you which sharps and flats to play. Think of the fingering you will use. Look to see if there are any scale or arpeggio patterns.

After giving yourself a minute or two to look at all these things, including the expression marks, play through the piece without stopping. Don't panic! Keep going, whatever happens, and play confidently.

22

23

24

25

26

27

28

29

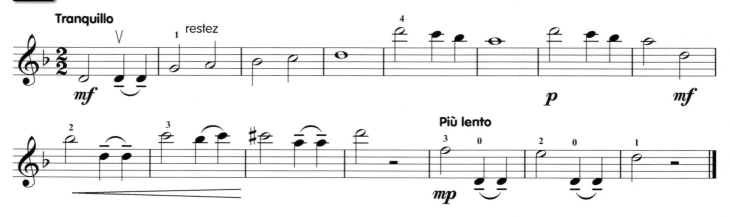

Solos

Follow the **TRaK**

33 **T** What does **C** stand for?

R Clap bars 4, 5, and 6, carefully noticing which quavers are dotted.

K Which bar has the notes of the arpeggio in?

! Play the 2 octave scale of B major. B♭ major and B major share the same finger pattern, so playing in 5♯s is not difficult.

Have your 4th finger ready as you play through firmly.

34 **T** How many minim beats in the bar?

R What rhythm is typical of a **Pavane**?

K Name the sharps in B major.

Watch the rests as you play through slowly, but dance-like. The bowing will help give the right feeling.

! Keep the linked bowing light and make sure you prepare 4th fingers.

Duets

35 *What does **Pesante** mean? Keep this rhythmical – the accents will help.*

Prepare 4th fingers in bars 4, 6, 8, and 11. Note the changes of time signature. Don't be caught out by the three bars of 4/4 near the end.

Pesante

Solos

Follow the **TRaK**

36

T Look carefully! What happens at bars 14 and 16?

R Clap from bar 10 to the end to help with the changes of time.

K B minor has the same key signature as which major?
Play the scale of B harmonic minor before you try this piece.

Play rhythmically, emphasizing the changes of time signature.

! Watch out for the 3rd finger A# in bar 6.

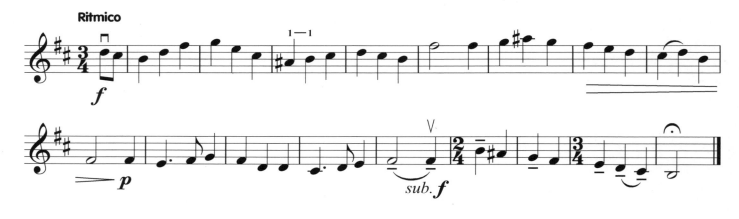

37

T Where is there a change of time signature?

R Clap carefully! Say the note names.

K Note all the bars with accidentals.

Play through in a spirited manner.

? Where is there a shift and what note do you shift to?

Duets

38 *How many changes of time signature are there?*

When playing through, let the music flow, and always listen to the 2nd part.

Solos

Follow the **TRaK**

39

T How many beats in a bar and what sort are they?

R Clap bars 9 and 10 before deciding on a speed.

K What is the key signature of E major? Play the 2 octave scale.

Look ahead to prepare finger patterns as you play through with a beautiful tone.

? Where do you shift into 4th position and where do you return to 1st position?

40

T What is the time signature? Why does the last bar of the **Minore** section have three and a half beats?

R Watch for the syncopation.

K What is the key signature of the major section and what of its tonic minor?

Play the one octave scales of E major and E minor, starting in 4th position on the A string before playing the piece.

! On a second play through, try putting the 1st section up an octave, in 4th position, using the same fingering.

26

Duets

41 *Let this sing with a beautiful tone, using a little vibrato on the longer notes.*

Prepare the fingers for the 1st bar before you start. What finger will you play E with?

E minor and 4th position

Solos

Follow the **TRaK**

42

T What is the time signature? Note the rit. and octave jumps in this piece.

R Which bars have a dotted rhythm?

K Which bar tells you that the key is E minor? Be careful of the accidentals when playing.

! Be ready for the shift into 4th position in the penultimate bar.

Keep this moving even though it is slow and broad. Use vibrato on the longer notes.

? What does **Largo** mean?

43

T What is the time signature? How many beats do you count on the last note?

R Hold the ties for their full value.

K Play the two octave scale of E minor, placing the D sharps carefully. What fingering do you use for the 2nd octave?

Play very expressively, thinking about how much bow to use on each note.

! Watch for the shift to 4th position at the end of bar 8.

Duets

44 *Add your own expression marks. How does the music make you feel?*

! In bar 10 watch for the semitone between B and C (2nd finger)

Tranquillo

Solos

45

T How many bars have semiquavers?

R Keep the rhythm lively.

K Find the 2 bars with dominant 7ths in them.

? What key are they in? Remember to stretch the 3rd finger G♯.

Play this in a cheeky fashion but be ready for the string crossing in bar 7.

! Choose a sensible tempo. Don't start too fast!

Allegretto giocoso

46

T What is the time signature?

R Look at the bars with semiquavers before deciding on a speed.

K What is the key? Don't be put off by the accidentals!

This should feel light and dance-like.

? Which bars have dominant 7ths?

Courante

crescendo al fine

Duets

47 *What does **Vigoroso** mean? How many dominant 7ths can you spot?*

Keep rhythmical and don't be put off by the chromatic notes in the 2nd part. Both players need to look at the accidentals before playing.

Which section should be played in 3rd position? Where does it shift back to 1st position?

Vigoroso

Solos

48

T Is the tempo the same all the way through?

R Name the notes as you clap through i.e. G A♭ A B♭ (beef) etc.

K What is the key?

Play firmly and steadily, placing the fingers carefully.

! Play a chromatic scale on G before trying this piece.

49

T Take a steady speed at first.

R Look at bars 2, 3, 4, and 6 before you play through.

K Try a chromatic scale on A before you start.

*What does **Agitato** mean?*

! Look carefully at the chromatic notes and linked bowing before you try to play!

Duets

50 *Find the dominant 7ths and check the chromatic fingerings before playing through without stopping.*

*Or 1 2 1 2 3 4

Solos

Although there are no hints to help you through the following pieces, keep checking the TRaK.

51

52

53

54

55

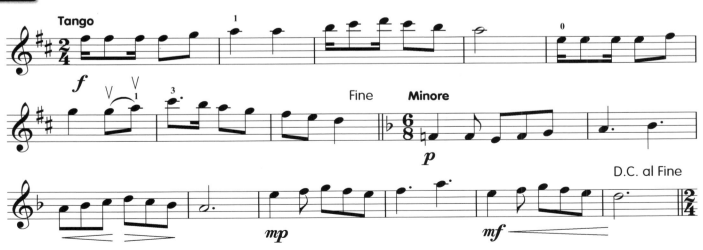